Lehi's Dream

written by Tiffany Thomas
illustrated by Nikki Casassa

CFI · An imprint of Cedar Fort, Inc. · Springville, Utah

HARD WORDS:
dream, fruit, building, river

PARENT TIP: Repetition is the key to learning and remembering new sight words. Your child may need to see a new sight word many times before they recognize and remember it.

Lehi has a dream from God.

It is
very dark.

Lehi walks
for a
long time.

3

Lehi finds a tree.
The tree
has good fruit.

Lehi calls his sons to eat the fruit.

Nephi and Sam say yes.
The others say no.
Lehi gets sad.

There is an
iron rod and
a path that
go to
the tree.

People hold onto the iron rod.
It gets dark.

There is a bad river and
a building with bad people.

Some people go away
from the path and get lost.

Some people hold onto the rod and get to the tree.

The iron rod is the word of God.
The fruit is the love of God.

The end.

ISBN 13: 978-1-4621-4337-5

Published by CFI, an imprint of Cedar Fort, Inc. • 2373 W. 700 S., Suite 100, Springville, UT 84663
Distributed by Cedar Fort, Inc., www.cedarfort.com

Cover design and interior layout design by Shawnda T. Craig
Cover design © 2022 Cedar Fort, Inc.
Printed in China • Printed on acid-free paper
10 9 8 7 6 5 4 3 2 1